April 15/1990

To Mrs. _____,

In appreciation _____

devotion to your Sunday

School class

Lans Hirschfeld.

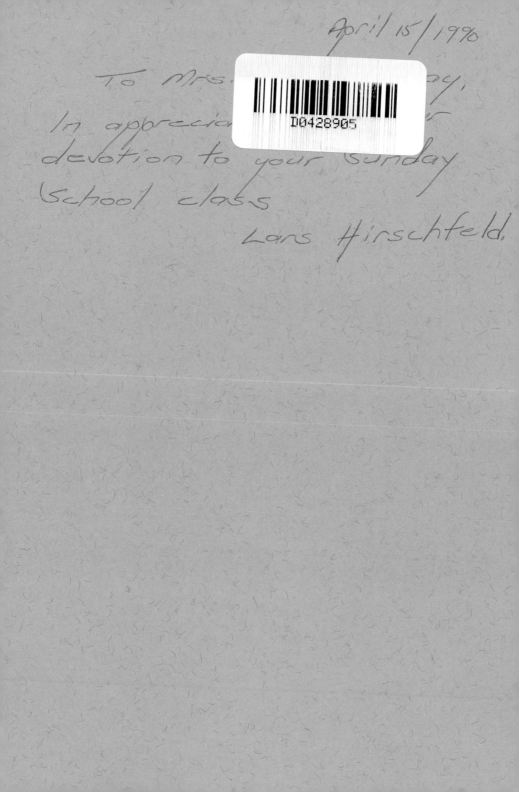

DEAR GOD
What Religion Were the Dinosaurs?

Dear God

What Religion Were
the Dinosaurs?

MORE CHILDREN'S
LETTERS TO GOD

DAVID HELLER

Illustrated by John Alcorn

Doubleday
NEW YORK LONDON TORONTO SYDNEY AUCKLAND

PUBLISHED BY DOUBLEDAY

a division of
Bantam Doubleday Dell Publishing Group, Inc.
666 Fifth Avenue, New York, New York 10103

DOUBLEDAY and the portrayal of an anchor with a dolphin
are trademarks of Doubleday, a division of
Bantam Doubleday Dell Publishing Group, Inc.

LIBRARY OF CONGRESS CATALOGING-IN-PUBLICATION DATA

Dear God, what religion were the dinosaurs? : more children's letters to
God / [compiled by] David Heller.—1st ed.
   p. cm.
1. God.   2. Children—Religious life.   3. Imaginary letters.
I. Heller, David.
BT102.D333 1990
231—dc20   89–32036
                                                   CIP

ISBN 0-385-26127-6

March 1990

FIRST EDITION

BG

*To my good friend and former
roommate at Harvard, Dave Johns,
whose own fine sense of humor
is a joy to all those who know him.*

*To my lovable and precocious
nephew, Carey Heller,
age five.*

*And to all of Carey's future
cousins who should happen to
call me "Daddy."*

Contents

Introduction

How do children imagine God? What would they say if they could speak or write to God? What youthful advice would they offer? Is there anything in the universe they would like to see God change?

These are some of the many questions about children that stir my curiosity and prompt me to investigate the religious notions of our smallest prophets. They speak about faith with great honesty and feeling, but their light-hearted commentary about how the world works is just as fascinating. In my previous books, *The Children's God*, *Talking to Your Child About God* and *Dear God: Children's Letters to God*, I have shared some of my early discoveries about the wit and wisdom of youngsters, ages four to twelve. Children do indeed have an inner spiritual life of their own, and my work has been an effort to make that inner life more accessible to the adult world in general and to parents in particular.

Dear God: What Religion Were the Dinosaurs? is a sequel called for by the enthusiasm for my first book of children's letters. This book continues in the spirit of its predecessor and extends its humor to a wider range of subjects. It is also an effort at furthering the inspirational message of my work.

In addition to such topics as family life, school, church or synagogue and their immediate friendships, children also correspond to God about different religions and cultures. They wonder about God's role in human history and ponder such interesting questions as: "Are miracles really possible?" Some of the children's letters reflect a curiosity about their ancestry as well as their understanding of age and time. They surmise that God may be a good One to ask about these weighty subjects. So they look to God for answers, direction and even a little comfort and understanding.

But not all the children's letters are about faraway

subjects. Many youngsters want to speak to God about
personal matters. They want to know about such things as:
"How can a kid be very happy?" and "Is a kid free to choose
things on his own?" When they ask God about these matters,
they are not only up-front and sincere, the children are
downright colorful. Their letters are something for all of us
to appreciate and enjoy.

   Dear God: What Religion Were the Dinosaurs? is a collection of childhood humor, but it is also a panorama of
children's philosophy of life. There is considerable insight
into the child's heart and mind in their original letters, along
with a hilarious glimpse into the trials and joys of growing
up. While these letters to God may sometimes sing with
youthful levity, they also mirror life with artful and un-
canny simplicity—just as their young authors do in the
spontaneous way they love and learn.

                                        David Heller
                                        Boston, Massachusetts

Dear God.
What Countrie Has
Produced the Most
Angels?

God,

My heroes are You, Martin Luther King, Chris Columbus, and Ghost busters.
    You are my second favorite. Honest.

                                        Melanie.
                                        (age 7)

Dear God,

Did you help the Geeks build the big stadeums or did they ruin it by themselves?

                                        No problem,
                                        Rodney
                                        (age 9)

To the Lord,

How come you have not helped women more threw the years. Persons like Joan of Arch and the witches in Boston?

                                        How come?
                                        Claire
                                        (age 10)

Dear God,

I like to read about you. I feel you are neat. I also like to read about people like Nat Poleon, Adolph Hitler and Musselslini.
    I think they may have been on the other side thou.

                                        Take it easy,
                                        Billy
                                        (age 10)

Please send this to God,

Hello God. I have a question for you. Is that all right? In all
the work you do, what was your favorite time of history. In
the beginning. Prehistoric. the 1960s. Or now??

> Let me know & thanks,
> Francine
> (age 11)

Dear God,

Did you watch the stuff about the Irans and the Cotras on
TV? What did you think? I thought that the stuff was mostly
not so legal.

> Best wishes,
> Charles
> (age 10)

Dear God,

I hope that you are looking after my family, and my state
(Coneticut) and my country (USA) and my planet (its earth).
And please take care of other people too. Where ever they
live.

> Sincerly
> Todd B.
> (age 11)

Dear God.

If you control all of time does that mean that you dont have to wear a watch. You should have a watch with latin numbers on it.

Amanda
(age 11)

Dear God,

Please explain these things to me. You can have 15 minutes on each.

1. Why do we have war?
2. Why are you invisibal?
3. Can a person have more than 1 life?
4. How did you make light?

Don't look at any body's elses answers please.

Okay?
Valerie
(age 11)

Dear God!!

Stop the world. I want to get off. And come back later. I am good with computers so I would be good for the future.

Orson
(age 12)

Dear GOD.

If you get mixed in with choosing our next president make sure there is a big scandal about George Bushes. He is boring.

Lizzie
(age 12)

Dear God.

Did Betsy Ross wear lipstick and makeup or were you against that in her day? What made you liberated afterward. Did you see the light.

I'm glad,
Mindy
(age 9)

God:

Hi. I would like to find out about some things from you. Could you tell me about why there is so many famous Jacksons. There is Michael Jackson, Reggie Jackson, German Jackson, Rev. Jackson and Janet Jackson.

I was just learning in school some thing that made me think of this. Did President Andrew jackson have a big family or what?

Please write when you can,
Shirley
(age 12)

Dear God,

Did you have to take American history too? I hate it. We learned about the part about Banker hill and all that stuff. Every person was big for money then too.

> Your friend,
> Anthony
> (age 11)

Dear God.

Why did you let Rome get away with so much?

> Fred
> (age 9)

Dear God,

I have a present for you.

It's a picture of Moses and the ten commands. Next time I will do St. Tom Aqinas.

> Sue
> (age 9)

Dear God,

I was sad to read about all the slaves in America. It was a long time ago. Maybe even 30 years.
     Don't hold this against us.

> Sylvia
> (age 8)

God,

Do things get better with each centurys or do they get bad
and even worst? Whats your plan?
    If they are supposed to get to being better, how do you
figure war. And television too?

                                            This is my letter,
                                            Dan
                                            (age 10)

Dear Lord.

Was the bible the first book? Or did the cavesmen make up
stories too.

                                            Your friend,
                                            Kev
                                            (age 9)

Dear god,

Thanks for giving us the sky and the animals and the
oceans. Thanks for new creations like computers. What will
be your next item?

                                            Merry christmas,
                                            Larry
                                            (age 9)

Dear god,

I wish there would be no more wars. If there is, I wish I could
live in space.

                                            Jean
                                            (age 10)

Dear God,

Was your wife involved in all the creating at the beginning or did she come in later on?

> Luv to all,
> Jennifer
> (Age 9)

Dear God,

Thank you for making the United States of America. You and George W. should be very proud. Gods and presidents should stick together, I think.

> John
> (age 8)

Dear God.

What countrie has produced and made the most angels?

> How are We doing?
> Celeste
> (age 7)

Dear GOD,

You must be very mad at us since we had two big wars in the last 100 years or something.
    Dont give up on us. There is still time in the next 13 years.

> Love,
> Edith
> (age 10)

Dear god,

Was Jesus really Jewish? I heard that he might have con-
verted.

Beth
(age 7)

Dear God!

Do you have your own flag?
I recommend this one.

clouds → [flag drawing] ← lightning

Every person would salute!

Eddie
(age 9)

Dear God,

I believe most of what I hear about you. Believe it or not. But
I am not so sure about one thing. I want to know if you can
truly make the sun stand still. And not move.

I thought it was corny and not really possible. When I
found out about it.

At the least it could not happen in this modern day and
ages.

Love,
Francine
(age 9)

Dear God.

You are number 1 in my heart and the most famous person in history that I can think of.

> God Bless you God.
> Edith
> (age 7)

To My God,

You are my friend. I know you was Jesuses friend too. We should be nice to friends. We should not crucify them. Unless we have a good reason.

> Your friend,
> Eddie
> (age 8)

Dear God,

If the people in Egypt were so bad, why didnot you get rid of all those pyramedes and sfinxes. Was it tough to move them? Try a bull dozer.

> The advice is free.
> Clayton
> (age 10)

Dear God, Did You Hear?

The russians and us might destroy some missiles. I don't think it will work. They can still use other boms and tanks and war ships. So can we. I think you should try a big meeting on a neutral cloud some where.

> Clark
> (age 11)

Dear God,

Why do so many persons who begin with I fight in wars.
Iranians. Iracs. Israel. Indians. You name it. Is it just an
accident? Maybe you should check on it. It gives all the I
people a bad name!

> Best wishes,
> Ingrid
> (age 9)

Dear GOD.

I want to know what the biggest 5 happenings is.

> This is my vote.
>> You created us.
>> Moses and the people took off.
>> Jesus was born.
>> The people landed on Plymouth Rocks.
>> You lost control of us.

> Is this right?
> Dave
> (age 10)

God,

Howdy. How is it by you? I am here in 1989 wondering what
is going to happen in the next few years. How about a sneak
preview?
    What I want to no is—will I have to go into the army?

> Your great,
> Jerome
> (age 9)

Dear God,

Do you flip out when they invent things like the car and the plane. Not the way you planned things in the chariott days. Huh? Wait till you see what we got next. I bet we are going to find a computer that can predict the future. Dont sweat though. You are still out of this world.

> Love,
> Tony E.
> (age 10)

Dear God,

I have read most of the Bible. I think you must be one of the greats of writing of all time. My teacher thinks Shakesbeare is the best. She is wrong. He never did nothing like floods and bushes and striking people dead and bringing them back to life. He was like a text book in school.

You sure wrote a lot. Did you get anybodies to type for you?

> I am learning to type,
> Ray
> (age 11)

Dear God,

You are king. The rest of us are like nites and servers. If I am good I want to visit your castle.

> Leslie
> (age 8)

God,

When did you first create pets for people? Was it early in
your creatin?

My dog Clyde is ok but he is real, real, lazy. He could not
have hacked it in the desert days.

Luv,
Sandy
(age 9)

Dear Sir.

I am pleased to write to you and ask you to remember me in
your prayers.

I would also like to find out if you have always looked
the same. Can you change your form.

What I mean is maybe you used to have a beard and
mostash a long time ago.

I will remember you,
Clay
(age 11)

Dear God,

Thanks for all the memories I had in my life. You must have
a lot of notebooks to keep track of what happened to everybody.

So long for now,
Les
(age 9)

2

Dear God, What Religion Were the Dinosaurs?

Dear God,

Which of Joseph's brothers did you favor? Was it Ben?
　　Do you like older brothers or younger brothers better
mostly?

> Your reliabal friend,
> Ben
> (age 9)

Dear God,

Is the world thousends of years old? If it is what religion
were the dinosaurs?
　　By the way, what happened to them. Did you get mad at
them and end them.

> What religion were they,
> Terry
> (age 10)

Dear God,

Did you like it when you were six? I guess it was ruff. You
need a rest after you was six. Me too.

> Luke
> (age 6½)

Here's a Letter For You, God

$$G$$

It is a romans number which shows how old you must be!

Darrell
(age 11)

Dear God,

Why did you make bar mitzvahs at when you are thirteen.
I bet it's since 13 is unlucky and you wanted to prove it
by making us learn all this stuff in hebrew.

A mesage from hebrew school,
Marshall
(age 12)

Dear Great One,

Now that I am ten I want to have a talk with you, please. I am
just about a hole decade. And you may not believe this, but I
have never been water skiing.
I think it is Time. Tell my dad to loosen up.

Love,
Cheryl
(age 10)

Dear Jesus,

Happy birthday a little late to you. I am writing you on Janurary 17.
I hope your birthday was good and you got as many presents as you gave.
That must be 1,986 for you. Far out!

> Anthony
> (age 9)

Dear God,

How old are you? You must be over the hill. Or is it over the mountain?

> Your buddy,
> Pete E.
> I'm eight.
> (age 8)

Dear God, Jesus and The Holy Spirit.

Did Adam really live for 900 years! If he did all the life insurance people must have wanted to cover him.

> Just joking,
> Tim
> (age 10)

Dear God,

To be a god how old do you have to be? Do you have to be over 50? One other question. Does a decade seem like a second to you. What do you think of the 1980s?

> Love always,
> Denise
> (age 11)

Dear God,

7, 000, 000, 000, 000, 000 000, 000, 000, 000, 000 000, 000, 000, 000, 000. That's how old, you must be! I used 7 becus I know you like that number.

Carl
(age 8)

Dear God,

My brother is mean. He says I am dumb because I am a kid (I am 8). My question is, did you do dumb things when you were a kid. Maybe a flood or a tornado or destroy a country?

I would really like an anser,
William
(age 8)

Dear God,

I am a boy. You need to know that to help. My girl friend Fran is 1 year older. Do you think it is okay?
   Her mom does not know about us.

Thank you,
Bryan
(age 8)

Dear God,

I read how you partered the red ocean. That was cool and unbelevable. How come you don't do things spectakquler like that any more. Hard to get up the energy?

Dan B.
(age 12)

Dear God (He or She),

I have a sister who is 23 years old and still in school! Can you beleive it. Please help her to graduate soon.

Best wishes,
Marsha
(age 9)

Dear God,

Why didn't you make parents closer to us kids in age. That way they can understand us better and would not yell at us so much.

    I think people should have babies when they are about 14.

Love,
Kim
(age 10)

Dear God,

My family has moved around since I was 4. It is nice to know that there is someone like You who is always there with us. Through the years.

Your friend,
Arn
(age 11)

To who it may concern,

I've been looking for you in church and don't see you anyweres. If you are real then tell me how old I will be when I get married.

We will see,
Carol
(age 9)

Dear God,

I think you and Jesus are the best. I heard that Jesus was your only begotten son. I cannot understand for the life of me (like my dad says) why you did not permitt him to live longer than age 33.

Other than that I believe in you with no questions asked.

Alex
(age 11)

Dear God ....

I put all the dots for a reason. I read that you go in finite and never come out again.

It makes my head hurt to think about you.

. . . . .
John J. Davis
(age 11)

God,

Who do you be long to. Kids or Grownups. You have to pick 1. No halfses.

With flowers,
Wendy
(age 6)

Dear God.

Were you there when Doctor Ruth was born. Boy that was a long time ago.

Don't giggle,
Ellen
(age 9)

Dear God,

We have ten tons of fun down here on the land. You should visit us more. We even have a home for the old people so you would feel right at home. But they are not rich homes like you must have in heaven.

Maybe you would not like it that much.

Will
(age 11)

Dear God

Time keeps on slippin to the future.

You better keep track.

Be bop hop,
Tina
(age 9)

Dear God,

By the time this reaches you I may even be in high school. But if it gets to you sooner I would like it if you would make fifth grade easier.

Thanks,
Edgar
(age 10)

Dear God, Who is forever

What do you do to stay young?

> What's your secret,
> Samantha
> (age 8)

Dear God,

How long did it really take you to make the first people? Do you feel you rushed too much?

> Keith
> (age 10)

To Mr. God.

Oh, you are wonderful to me. I love you like I love Grandpa McIntyre. Are you gray too?

> Luv,
> Tammy
> (age 7)

God,

I heard that in the bible (pretty much in the beginning), a man named Abrahamm and a lady named Sara had a kid when they was reel old. Reel old. I liked that because my mom and dad were reel old when they had me. They were 30 years each when I was born.

> I have been very good,
> Kate
> (age 8)

Dear God.

COMING ATTRACTIONS.
   I will be nine soon. I am ready to be let in on how life works. Also please make sure I have a good birthday.

Love,
Sue
(Almost Age 9)

To what ever rules us,

I'm not sure if I believe in you at all, but in case I do, such as when I'm old, I figured I'd write you just the same.

Marty
(age 9)

Dear God,

You should have people live till theyre a hundred. That way they can really tell all the younger ones about all the changes.

Love,
Celia
(age 10)

Dear God,

How do you organize things the way you do? Did you ever think to make Jacob older than Abraham and putting him first?

Hello,
Bill T.
(age 12)

Dear god.

I wonder if you have the same problems people do. Do you have to worry about money and do you have to save up there for when its time to go to college?

Thank you.
Diana
(age 10)

God,

How come you measured everythings in cubes in the Bible?
    What did you do for things that was a different shape than a cubit.

Sean
(age 11)

Dear One True God,

Is it true that people used to have kids when they were old. Man they must get awful gray. I hope they had grownup kids to keep an eye on them.

I admire you.
Betty
(age 9)

Dear Lord,

What did noahs arch look like?
Was it a big old ship?

Love,
AMY
(age 9)

Dear Jesus,

When you said that you have to be a little kid to make it to heaven, did you really mean it? I mean do you have to be like ten years old and act real respectful to your elders?

> I am just about ten,
> Ronald
> (age 9)

Dear God or Jesus, Who ever is not too busy. I believe in being a Christian very much. Even when I am sixteen and can drive and all grown up. I will have faith.

> LOVE,
> Karen
> (age 8)

BIG G,

Hi out there! I got only 1 request. MORE RIGHTS FOR 9 year olds. I am sick of hearing about wait till you're ten.

> George
> (age 9)

Dear God,

You are all right and okay even if you are not a kid. Maybe you were at one time.

> Melanie
> (age 7)

3

Dear God, Keep the Generations Rolling!

Dear God,

How is your eyesight? Do you wear glasses? My grandfather
does when he reads.
    Also I want to find out if you wear a robe at night. Does
it have a monogram on it?

Peace,
Patti
(age 10)

God,

I think you must have a big throne up there in heaven with
lots of flowers around. Like Daisies. I think all the old people
must be next to you. They must have Old flowers around.
Like trees.

Eva
(age 8)

Dear God,

If I could get you a present I would buy you a huge wooden
rocking chair. That way you can relax every day when you
are done saving people and feeding them.

Warm wishes,
Tamara
(age 10)

Dear God,

With all the relatives you have, how do you get everyone together for Thanksgiving and Xmas?

Mark
(age 9)

Dear Lord,

Were Jesus and Solomon related or do they just live near each other. Do you know from memory or do have to check a list?

I'll be good,
Steven
(age 8)

Dear God,

What does the word begat mean in the Bible. They certainly used it a heck of alot.

Pardon my grammer,
Dom
(age 9)

For God,

I want you to check something for me. I want to know who my great, great, great, great grandpaents were. Was it ben franken and his wife?

I'll be waitin,
Loren
(age 10)

Dear God,

I worry about you since you must not have a family the way
we do. You must get real alonelee.
    How about sharing my family? They argue a lot but they
are good to have mostly.

                                        With Love,
                                        Ann Marie
                                        (age 7)

Dear god.

Did all the guys in the hole world come from that guy adam
or it that just a fairys tale?
    Was about that eve girl?

                                        Yours trulys.
                                        James
                                        (age 9)

Dear Father,

The earth is yours and every last thing in it. I want to say
thanks for letting us rent it.

                                        April
                                        (age 11)

Dear God, Lord and Savior.

I wish I could have been there when you got up from the dead
back there in the Bible days. That would have been a great
thing to brag about to my friends.
    But I guess I would not be around today if I was there in
your day.

> Bless me please,
> Paul
> (age 9)

Dear God,

I think of you in my prayers. Along with my mom and my
dad, my sister Paula, my grandma, my two grandpas, my
aunt Jenie, my aunt Gloria, my uncle Sid, my uncle Jack and
my cousins Billy and Sherie.
    I spend at least 3 minutes on you *every* night!

> Love,
> Terry
> (age 8)

Dear God,

Why are grandparents so much nicer than parents? Is it
their experience or is it they just give up being mean?

> Hello,
> Jamie
> (age 12)

God.

Was I ever related to a gorilla? You know. Like King Kongs.
I don't buy that science stuff.

Hawkeye
(age 9)

God,

Are you there. I see you as like a big grandfather clock that
is real steady and keeps on ticking. Even in water.

Merry Christmas,
Joe
(age 11)

Dear God,

Who is *your* mom and dad?
The reagans?

Bye bye,
Tricia
(age 8)

Dear God,

Do you consider Adam your son or is He like an invention.
Which is it?

All yours,
Kenneth
(age 10)

Dear God,

My grandfather died this year, as you know. I felt very sad.
Maybe you did not know.
   My grandfather likes ice cream a lot. Please make sure
he is taken care of.

> Your friend,
> Ian
> (age 6)

Dear God.

Do you look like the guys on the Bottles and james commer-
cials or do you look like a normal old person?

> Charlene
> (age 10)

Dear God,

How many generations has it been since Old Abraham in the
Bible and his family? Have you lost count?

> Hello God.
> SaM
> (age 8)

Dear God

I read where people used to sleep more than you do now.
Where you involved in changing things. Why change a good
idea?

> Please answer,
> Marie
> (age 10)

Dear God and Grandma,

Hi. I want to write you in Heaven. I want you to know that I am going to be a television star like I told you about.

God, I miss grandma but I am glad she is keeping you companie.

Love and kisses,
Elizabeth
(age 11)

Dear God,

I would like to know about the 12 disciples of Jesus. Could you send me some facts about their families and their jobs. Even Judas.

Thank you,
Carla
(age 9)

Dear God,

I want to tell you how much I love you. You are a lot like my uncle Nat. He is kind and generous.

Other kids and even grown ups are in title to have their own views. That is okay. Everybody has a rite to make their own mistakes.

Your humble letter
riter,
Byron
(age 12)

Dear GOD—

You can be bigger than my dad. Whew. that is a lot of big.
    I am excited. Please do not step on me by accidant.
Please. I am very small.

> Michelle
> (age 7)

Dear God,

In summer time do you relax in the garden in a big ham-
mock and eat fruit. That is what my grandfather does. But
he does not have a garden. He thinks that is sissy stuff. He
has a backyard.

> Take it easy,
> Al
> (age 9)

God,

I have been meaning to right you. I just could not find the
time. Sorry. I want to say hi. I also want to ask you if my
family and parents are from famous people.
    I mean like Noah and the animals on the Ark.

> Love,
> George
> (age 10)

Dear God,

How do you find time to visit all your grandkids? Santa Claus has a sled but how do you get around. Maybe you don't need one.

> Corinne
> (age 8)

Big letter to god.

Keep the generations rollin!

> Alex
> (age 10)

Dear God.

I read some where where you know what we are going to do before we do it. How much advance notice do you get?

> I would like to know,
> Sheila
> (age 10)

Dear God:

Hi. Up in the sky. Up hi. Why. Guy. Shy. I don't lie. Ni. Not at all guy. Guy in the sky.
    Bye.

> I will write you again
> when I am a big poet
> and I have grandkids,
> Lauren
> (age 11)

Lord,

Three things I pray. Honor you more nearly. Worship you more fairly. And write you more than once a year.

I guess religious persons skip a generation in my family. That's what my mom says. I will try harder.

Don't be cross,
Paul
(age 11)

Dear God,

Here are all my relatives.

I am the 5th one. The one with the halo.

Jay
(age 9)

Dear God,

I have some relatives who live far away in Israel. I do not get to see them much. But I Know You Are Everywhere. You can travel in seconds. So please watch over them (they live near Jerusalem). Let me know how they are doing and tell them my little league team finished in first place.

I will write them about it soon.

I would appreciate it,
Stuart
(age 11)

Dear God,

My name is Dave. I am a dissendent of King David David. He played the harp. I play an instrument too. I play the drums. I want to be king of music.

Love,
Dave S.
(age 12)

To My God,

Do you know my grandmother? She is very sick with cancer and other stuff. Please make her better and I will do a lot of good things. I will help my little brother with his homework and not yell at him. I will not hit him much either.

Please help,
Bill
(age 12)

Dear God,

What I would like to know is when will the world end? I got time so you don't have to let me know right now. Please tell me a week before.
     I want time to pack.

Let me know.
Stanley
(age 11)

Dear God,

If you ran for President you would have a hard time getting
elected. You would have to promise a lot and not come
through.

Better wait till 2050. That group of people may be
different. You could get votes.

Richard S.
(age 10)

Dear God,

I think you must be very smart. It was a radical idea to make
all humans beings different colors and have them be from
different nations.

I guess it will get more colorful the more they mix
together. Is that how you planned it.

Tellis
(age 11)

Dear God.

You are father to us all. All of us. I like you too cuz I can spell
you. G O D.

Love.
Debra
(age 6)

Dear god,

I feel very close to you.
Like your my own relative or something.
Even closer.

With love,
Ian
(age 9)

4

Dear God,
My Mother and Father
Honk for Jesus and
Cars That Are in the
Way Too!

Dear Jesus,

When you talked to Moses and Elijah on the mountain what language did you speak? Was it a secret code language.

> I love you,
> Jerome
> (age 10)

Dear God.

When Jacob wresttled with the angel who got pinned?

> Curtis
> (age 12)

Dear God,

I know what you mean about that Giant Golias. Theres a big kid in my class whose a jerk too!

> I'm on your side,
> Stanley
> (age 10)

God,

What do you think of guys like Mohamud, Buuda and the others like them? I do not understand their ideas. But maybe you do.

> Raymond
> (age 12)

To God,

How do you know Satan when you see him? Can you give me any clues.

>Your loyal little girl,
>Charlene
>(age 9)

Dear God,

Can a person have two religions? If they do how do you decide on their fate at the end?

>Love,
>Camille
>I am a Catholic
>(age 8)

Dear God,

My friend Bob goes to a Church with these huge stained glass windows. Did you command some people to put this colored glass in their churches or is that one of their own ways of saying they are colorful?

>Best wishes,
>Jerry
>(age 11)

Dear god,

I want to tell you that I like you super lot. My family is Methodist. Please like us a super lot.

>Yours truly,
>Dawn
>(age 8)

Dear God,

What do you think about those scandals with the ministers on tv? What are you going to do to them. I would like to suggest that you send them to radio.

Sincerely,
Elgin
(age 9)

Dear GOD,

I think you were not hard as you should have been on Ponjo Pilot back there in Jesus's time. You should have got him and the other pagans good.

Unless you have more information about what happened to them after they died.

Get them good,
Richie
(age 11)

Dear God,

Does Jesus love all the kids of the world the most? That is what my uncle Phil says. He says its because all the others (except maybe persons over 70) worship business and materials.

There should be a religion of just kids. We could call it KIDS UNLIMITED. I volunteer to be president.

Love,
Len
(age 11)

Dear God,

Did you not like Messoptomaia because it was such a big Mess? Or because they were not Jewish?

> Tell me please,
> Marcie
> (age 9)

Dear God,

The best thing that you created off the top of your head was rainbows. I am glad you gave that to peoples of all religions and races and not just to persons who needed some sunshine.

> Your dedicated child,
> Annette
> (age 10)

To God.

Every religion has a Mr. Lot's girlfriend. But why did you turn her into salt.
That was mean.
You could have at least turned her into diamons.

> Laurie H.
> (age 9)

Dear God,

Take a Memo. Synagogue services are too long. please shorten them. The church people only have to go for an hour. Stop memo.

> Elissa
> (age 11)

Dear GOD,

How many religions are there? When you go through your list, do you figure out which ones have been naughty and which have been nice?

Sammy
(age 8)

Dear God,

Do you know how you have all the Mormons in Utah? You should have some religion that you *don't* like in New Jersey.

I am not saying Who,
(age 10)

Dear God,

Does Santa Claus visit you at Christmas or don't you believe in him anymore?

Merry XMAS,
Lori Ann
(age 7)

Dear God,

When you visit places that don't have real religions, like Washington D. C., you must come with bodyguards. I do not want anything to happen to you.

Jamie
(age 9)

GOD, GOD, GOD

> Christians, Jews and Catholics
> We are all alike
> We are all brothers
> Cause there sure aren't no others.

> > Your humble poet,
> > Carl
> > (age 12)

Dear GOD in heaven:

Be easy on the atheists people. They do not mean you no harm.

> > Jerrold
> > (age 8)

God,

I feel that human beings should treat you with more respect. Catholics, Protestant persons and Jewish people should be particulerly nice since they know you so much better.

> > Rhonda
> > (age 10)

Dear God,

You should change the rule on preists and nuns. So they can get married and have kids. Otherwise they get off scott free and can get lonely and get into trouble. I know. My uncle is a priest.

> > Hallelujah,
> > Bonnie
> > (age 10)

God,

They are trying a new thing in school. They are trying to teach us about the Buddas and the strange ideas from somebody whose name sounds like confused (confuses, I think).

I think they are trying to be too liberal. They should stick to bible stories and your commands.

Larry
(age 11)

Dear God,

How is an orthodox Jew different from a reformed Jew in your eyes. I am a Conservative Jewish person so I am not placing my bets on either.

Love,
Ronald
(age 12)

Dear God,

I remember when you got p.o.ed at the men and women at the Tower of Babel. What a big headache.

Is that why you have so many different people saying different things about who you is?

Thanks,
Theresa
(age 9)

Dear God,

What is your favorite religious book? Mine is Judy Blume's.

Sandy K.
(age 11)

Dear God,

What religion was Ishmel in the Bible? Was he Israeli or PLO?

Drew
(age 10)

Dear God,

My mom, dad and all of us worship you. But we have a dog named Rookie too. Is it all right if Rookie does not worship you. Rookie is not allowed in Church! Please understand.

Love,
Donald
Owner of Rookie
(Donald, age 9;
Rookie, age ?)

Dear Father,

What do you do when passover and easter are the same day? Hire a representative to cover all the homes?

Brent
(age 12)

Dear God,

My mother and father honk for Jesus and cars that are in the way too.

> Love and sweet thoughts,
> Cherie T.
> (age 8)

God,

I am an Armenian. Most of our names end in *ian*. So does yours. You are our Guard*ian*.

> Love,
> Seta
> (age 12)

Dear GOD,

Are there things we are still not supposed to do on the Sabbath? I don't know how to break this to you but the malls are open all day and every day. The people there don't rest. Some people go there instead of services.
     Sorry to bring this bad news to you, God.

> Don't be upset.
> Cary
> (age 11)

Dear God,

You sure used to have a lot of wise men all the time in the Middle East.
     What happened to them all?

> Warren
> (age 12)

God.

I think the saddest part of the Bible was when Kane knocked out Ables. But I want to know if he got a fair trial after it happened?

> Edmund
> (age 10)

Dear God.

Which of the commandmants are the biggest? Or are they all about the same for getting into troubles with you?

> Hello God.
> Leigh Ann
> (age 10)

Dear God,

I would like to know what you do on Sunday mornings. Do you do religious things or do you play tennis like my mom and dad?

> Alex
> (age 10)

Dear God,

Where do the bad people of all religions really go after they croak?
    Write me an answer or tell me but please do not send me pictures. I hate creature films!

> Your buddy and friend,
> Luke
> (age 9)

Dear God,

You need to visit my middle school. There ain't enough old time religion there. Plus we would probably get a day off for religion if you came.

Marlene
(age 9)

I want to ask God,

I know a kid who has a mother who is jewish and a father who is Protestant.
Did you hear about it?

Mitchell
(age 10)

For God,

Here is the most wanted list for me.
1. SATAN—your enemy.
2. JUDAS—he betrayed Jesus.
3. FAROH—the one Moses took on.
4. HERO—the king in Jesus time.
5. PILOTS—I forget what he did wrong.
SATAN is the one I am most against.

Yours truly,
Bob
(age 10)

Dear god,

How do you feel about arguing about religion beliefs or do
you stay away from getting into fights about politics?

                                        Matt
                                        (age 11)

Dear God, Did You Hear the One About the Minister Who Ran for President?

Dear Heavenly Father,

I want to find out. I mean I would like to know how you decide that a person will be your messenger. Do you get the stats out on them?

Henry
(age 12)

Dear God,

You should stop by and give a talk at our Church. I promise to go next Sunday if you are going to be there.
    O, how will I know its you?

With love,
Ashley
(age 10)

Dear Saint Augustine,

I am writing to you because I thought it might take too long to reach God. I need some help soon. My teacher Sister Mary has it in for me. I didn't do anything wrong. Honest.

Anthony
(age 9)

God,

I like everything just the way you created it. I think that the
people at Church who are against rock musicians are not
right. It must be okay with you or you would have killed it
from the beginning.

Pia
(age 8)

Dear God,

Do you know my minister, Rev. Head. We call him reverend
Deadhead!

I like writing this
letter,
Orren
(age 12)

Dear God, Sur Lord.

What are the Chinese religious big people called? Are they
emperors? Don't they have a hard time reading the Bible?
They have so many people it must be easy to get a full house
at Church.

Anna
(age 10)

Dear God,

Are you like a rabbi like they called Jesus? If the answer is
yes, I want to say that I like Jewish people even though I am
Protestant.

Yours truly,
Justin
(age 10)

Dear God,

Are preachers like ministers and priests? Are they close to you or do they just talk loud. I say put them in their places and have them stop taking your name in their veins.

Francis
(age 12)

Dear God,

How much do you pay the people who work for you? Do priests get vacation time?

I would like to know,
Joy
(age 8)

Dear Jesus,

I wish you were still around. That way you could walk on water or do whatever you feel like and we would not have to listen to boring sermons.

Adolpho
(age 10)

Dear God.

Is Mike Landon like a priest or is he just an actor?

That's my question,
Larry
(age 8)

God,

Like I said in confession. I am sorry. Please forgive me. And make sure Father Ryan keeps quiet about it.

Thank you,
Patrick
(age 11)

Dear God,

How come there are not more ministers and churches in the Bible. Were they a late brainstorm?

Martina
(age 9)

Dear God 〜〜〜〜

I go to Most Precious Blood school. Other kids make fun of us. They say our nikname is the Donors.
    We need a new name.

Respectful,
Dom
(age 10)

Dear GOD:

Can girls be ministers with the Protestant peoples?
    That must be how Amy Grant got so popular.

Best wishes.
Always
Crystal
(age 9)

God,

Every Christmas our church takes up a toy collection. We try our best. Last year I donnated a doll.

This year has been a hard year. It will have to be a set of jacks.

Sorry for the bad News.

Love anyway,
Teri
(age 10)

Dear God,

You are wonderful. You should be a priest or something!

Hilary
(age 8)

Dear God.

I heard a good joke that I bet you will love. It goes like this.

A priest and a minister and a rabbe were in a sinking boat. Only one could live. They tried to decide who would stay. Who was the biggest in importance. Finally they agreed that the priest and the rabbe would have to die. The minister could live in the yacht. Do you wonder why?

It was since the minister was most important since he was running for President!

Hope you like it,
Vic
(age 12)

DEAR GOD,

More people should dedicate theyre lives to you. That would
be cool. Then there would be more persons such as Mother
Theresa and other mothers. Like mine.

Love,
Barb
(age 9)

Dear God,

Why isn't Church services out doors? That way we can have
them under the lights like baseball games and get bigger
crowds. You can sell hot dogs and charge people too!

Don't sweat.
Ed
(age 10)

Attention: God.

Please tell Rev. Johnson to stop calling you a *him* every
single time he talks about you. Tell him youre a girl and set
him strait.

Best wishes,
Melissa Sue
(age 10)

Oh God,

My father is not very religious. My mom tries to get him to be. My minister says I should try to help. What should I do, God? I read about how every person has to decide alone. You and my minister and my mom must not be on the same wavelength.

Keith,
(age 12)

God,

I believe that you and Bishop Tutoo care the most of all the gods in the world. Bishop Tutoo has it rough because he is in southern Africa and there is lots of hate there.
Also his name sounds a little funny.

Bart
(age 11)

Dear God,

We took a picture at Sunday School but my minister did not come out. Do all your employees not come out in pictures. What is the reason for that. Do you want to be secret?

Frieda
(age 9)

Dear God,

I belong to CYO. I like it a lot. You should have more groups like that. How about BYO and GYO? That way we don't have to be nice to girls even if they are Catholic.

Forgive me Father,
Charles
(age 11)

For the Lord God,

God bless you and Father Thompson and Sister Rose and
Sister Catherine. Also please bless the rest of us. We try as
best we can to serve you even if we do not wear uniforms.

Mary Ellen,
(age 8)

Dear God,

I think you should listen to confessions in person. That way
bad people wouldnot try to get away with murder!

Hi,
George
(age 11)

Dear GOD,

Why was Moses' brother, Aren, the first high priest? Was it
a sure thing because he was taller or something like that.

Very truly.
Lorraine
(age 10)

Dear God,

I try hard to learn about you and also about my religion. My
minister is nice and he tries to teach all the kids about the
way to be.
    I guess some of us kids are hard headed types. So I hope
that your not in a big hurry for everybody to be perfect.

Love,
Anita
(age 11)

To God—

My dad is a deakun at our church so you must know who we
are. I want to be a deak too. So lets keep in touch.

> Best wishes and all that,
> Dave
> (age 11)

Dear God,

Thanks very much for giving me a great mom and dad. I am
very happy. I like the people in our neighborhood too. I also
like the people at the synogogue. Every one is nice. Even the
canter. He is the one who screems to loud.
   My question is, are you going to recrute more people to
be Jewish or are we just supposed to have a bunch of kids.

> What is new with you,
> Arthur
> (age 12)

Dear God,

Women should allow other girls to be priests and ministers.
So should be men. It is only fair. We can make people give to
the poor just as good as boys.

> With love,
> Anne
> (age 10)

Dear God,

I wish to find out if you have a vice God, like they have in Washington. I think it would be a good idea so he could run for God after you retire. Also in the mean time he could act like an angel and visit foreign contries and planets.

> With kindness,
> KIKI
> (age 11)

Dear God,

I go to a Catholic school now. Soon I will be a teenager and I should make choices for myself. No questions about it.

I am thinking that I'll be a priest. I would sure like you to kinda guide me.

Will I be able to stay away from girls?

> Bryan
> (age 12)

Dear God,

What type of religious leaders do they have in other countries? How do you keep track of them all? It must be a real big operation. But keep watching them and make sure they go out to their people and do a good job.

We need all the peace and love we can get.

> Alexandria
> (age 9)

To God,

Our minister is very sick with medical problems. Remember him in your prayers. He always speaks positive about you.

> I know he will be all right with
> your help,
> Cory
> (age 8)

Dear Father God,

I am writing to you about Father Welch who does a lot for the people here in my town. I think you should make him a pope or something. He is very good. But please move Rome to the U.S. so he can stay here with us.

> Love,
> Maureen
> (age 9)

Dear God,

I read in school about Saint Paul and Saint Francis and St. Andrew. My name is Loretta. If you want to honor a few more girls, I can be found at Saint Raphael's School. Saint Lor is fine.

> Love,
> Loretta
> (age 10)

Dear Lord:

The Bakers should no better. The PTA scandal is disgusting.

Nancy
(age 7)

Dear Friend,

When the High Priests were mean to Jesus, you should have court marshaled all of them.

That is my idea,
Donald
(age 9)

6

Dear God,
Was Samson and
the Haircut Thing a
Big Disappointment
to You?

Dear God,

I am 11. I heard at school that I will be going through a whole heap of change soon. All I ask is this. Please give me an advance warning.

Sheila
(age 11)

To Mr. God,

Why did you let men in the Old testament have so many wives? Was it *your* wish?

Hello,
Jen
(age 10)

Dear God,

Do you know this culprit?

Another one bites the dust,
Craig
(age 12)

Dear GOD,

Can you have a few bad thoughts and still be a saint? Just a
few. Honest.

> This letter is from James,
> who tries to be like
> saint James.
> (age 8)

Dear God,

I have a quiz for you like the bad ones we get in school. (I am
in the sixth Grade)
    What does Delilah, Samson's wife, Cleopatrick and
Alexia on Dynasty have in common?
    The answer is that all were teases and got guys into
trouble.

> Wayne
> (age 12)

Dear God,

When you socked it to Sadom and Gommorons what kind of
wicked things were the folks there doing?

> You can tell me,
> Andy Y.
> (age 10)

God,

When did you start clothing and pants and stuff? My mom told me the first people on the earth walked around in their birthday sutes. It must have been wierd for you to have to look at them all the time.

> Think of me in your prayers,
> Thomas
> (age 11)

Dear God,

I know that abortion is very evil but how did it get started to begin with?

> Pearl
> (age 8)

God,

What do you think about that mean guy in Panama? Do you know he sells drugs? Get rid of him. Thats what I say.

> Elliot
> (age 10)

Dear God,

I live in South Carolina. I want to thank you for helping me with troubles. I would like you to help me in your free time with my grades and my real tough teachers.

God I know your power and that you are strong too. Let me see more of that. Some people think that you are stupid and weak. But I don't. I know you have muscles.

> From Your Friend,
> Burt
> (age 10)

Dear God,

Thank you for allowing me to have the chance to dance for you.
    Now I could use some new ballet shoes if that is possible.

> Luv.
> Phyllis
> (age 12)

Dear God,

My dad had a talk with me about boys and girls. How they are different and all. I knew most of it already. You did a good job with that. Only maybe you should have had a third sex so we all had more of a choice.

> Love,
> Carlton
> (age 10)

Dear God,

The thing I wish I knew is where you go when you die. I can figure out what the older people do, but what on earth do kids do there?

> With a big kiss,
> Pamela
> (age 9)

Dear Jesus,

Do you think there are too many dirty tv shows and movies?
My minister thinks so.
    I just watch sports my self.

                              Trying to be the best,
                              Joe
                              (age 8)

To the Lord God,

My hero in the Bible was a girl named Esther. She even has
a hilday, Purim, named after her. You must know her. I have
always wondered if she was beautiful. Do you have an
old-fashoned picture of her I could see.

                              Your friend,
                              Maril
                              (age 10)

Dear God,

I always say I love you and worship you every single night
before I get into my bed. I mean it too. Please take good care
of me and don't let anything bad happen to me.
    I think my mom and dad would pray to you every single
night too but they are busy doing other things. Just about
every single night.

                              With a Hug,
                              Linda C.
                              (age 8)

Dear God,

I have been dying to ask you. Does each of us live only once.
Or do we have a couple of lives. If that is the way it is, are
girls always girls and boys always boys. If they are not, I am
impressed. It must be a real trick to do the change over.

Carmen
(age 11)

Dear God,

There should be a book about you. It would be a best seller.
They could have a big burning bush and a cross on the cover.

If that would not get the people, that would be on the
back and they would put a lady all dolled up on the front.
That works every time.

J. M.
(age 10)

Dear God

I know some things that we are not supposed to do. I will put
them in this box to show you.

Do not eat before Grace.
Do not talk back to elders.
Listen to our teachers.
Do not use bad language.
Do not talk about sex.
Do not get aids.

Dennis
(age 9)

To God on Mars.

I live on the planet earth. It is the home of President Reagan, Bill cosby and people like david letterman.
   You will want to visit here. We also have a girl named sibil sheperd.

Over and out,
Kyle
(age 9)

Dear God,

Do you believe in premarriage sex? My mother says it is not right but I hear it from a person with so much experience like you. I mean a God with so much experience.

Randy
(age 11)

God,

I like you and I like Glorie Steinum. Her magazine is good becuase she cares about women. Also, it does not have too much sex in it. I know you must be in favor of it.
   My girlfriend Anita says you might be a girl even though I always heard you were not. I hope you are a girl. It would be better.
   Since men are such dorks!

With love,
Angela
(age 10)

Dear God,

What were fig trees for in the Bible days? Did the kings and servants make out under them?

Just fooling,
Kenny
(age 11)

Dear God,

I love so much. I love you all the time. When it is raining I feel so good about you. I also like the sun and the warmth and all the leaves in autumn and all the other wonderful creations you made. Everything but stuck up flirty girls.

Johnny
(age 10)

Dear God,

My mother is very involved in the rights to life group. I am very proud of her. My question is how does a person know what good cause to get involved in? Let me know what to fight against.

Rita
(age 8)

G-D

I hope it is allright for me to write you this letter. We have it for an assinement. I would like to tell you that I never swear or do nothing bad. But its not true. So I won't even try to snow you.

Dean
(age 10)

Dear God,

Was Samson and the haircut thing a big disappointment to you?

Love,
Charlotte
(age 11)

Dear God,

If the men and the womens in the Bible were so holy how come they messed up so much and you had to punish them good.
I wish you didn't do this. My mom uses it to say it is okay to punish me.

I still like you,
John
(age 8)

Hi Heavenly Father!

We have been friends since I was a baby and maybe even earlier!

Jordan
(age 7)

Dear God,

I like Ally Sheedy because she is very pretty. Do you like pretty people best?

Please like me,
Delia
(age 11)

Dear God,

I am not sure if I am supposed to ask about this, but if you
don't mind, Lord, what were you thinking about when you
made sex?
I hope that it is okay to ask.

Love always,
Brooke B.
(age 12)

Dear God,

Who do you keep with you for company. I am just concerned
about you.

Dana
(age 8)

Dear GOD,

What exactly happens to a person who swears. Please let us
have a few screw ups.

Riley,
(age 11)

Dear God,

Please give us more sun here in Maine. But let us have
winter and lots of snow.

John
(age 7)

Dear God,

I just would like to ask you for some help if it is okay to use this letter to do that. Okay God?

I just found out that my eyes are not so good. I don't want to get glasses.

Please help me to get better and make my eyes good.

Love,
Mira
(age 8)

Special delivery to God

Why not have a few new comandmants.
How about one that goes—

Thous should not have to wash dishes until you are big and older and have a family or two of your own.

Think about this,
Stephanie
(age 12)

Dear God,

Why does being Jewish go by what mothers are? My mom told me that and I don't see why.

Are you sexist or what?

Sharon
(age 12)

Dear God,

What was the rest of the story with jesus and mary magad-
alana? What went on there. I would like to know.

> Hope you do not think I
> am a busy buddy,
> Cheryl Z.
> (age 9)

For God,

What do you watch on the 4 of July? you watch our fire-
works or do you make your own?

> Have a good rest of the summer,
> Alicia
> (age 10)

To God,

I want to thank you for the good things. That you have given
us. Like ice cream. Toys. Baseball. And girls at the beach.

> Steve
> (age 12 going on 19)

Dear God,

I never really thought about writing you but it kind of hit me all of a sudden.

God, could you please give me better looks? If you can't don't worry about it.

Everythings okay here I suppose but the school could use a little more anointing.

> Love always until the
> hour I am with you,
> Stephanie
> (age 11)

God

From Study Hall

When I grow up I want to a have beautiful wife and a cute son. I want to play football for the Denver Broncos. I would be good to everybody and not be too violent and mean against the other teams.

> Vernon
> (age 10)

Dear God,

Did you make aids because there is too much loose sex or because you thought the world needed a new disease.

> Randall
> (age 11)

Dear God,
Do You Help Mrs. Fields
Make Chocolate Chip
Cookies?

Dear God,

I want to know what you look like and what things you do.
For example first—Do you start wars? Do you make peace?
Do you eat 3 meals a day?

> I do,
> Charlotte
> (age 8)

Dear God,

What do you stain from during Lent? I am a Catholic and we
keep from things chewing gum and potato chips.
    Maybe you should keep from having people die this
year.

> An idea from Curt
> (age 10)

Dear Mr. God,

Do you get drunk on wine like the men in the Bible? My dad
drinks too much too. So do not feel bad or sad. You are not
alone.

> Your buddy,
> Andrew
> My dad's name is Phil
> (age 9)

Dear God,

What do *you* eat? Do you have to eat? If you don't you must think all the people on diets are pretty stupid.

                                        Hi,
                                        Deron
                                        (age 8)

For God,

Why not try the gardens of edens again? Ever thought about it.

     This time you could try it with out the apples and snakes.

                                        Very best wishes to you,
                                        Kim
                                        (age 10)

Dear Mister God,

I think you should have made all the roads out of gingerbread and all the telephon polls out of candy canes. That way the world would be sweet and no babies would go hungry.

                                        Love,
                                        Afton
                                        (age 7)

Dear God,

Dont let the devil have any water. That way he cant put out any fires down there. And he will get plenty thirsty too.

                                        Dick
                                        (age 8)

Dear God in the Bible,

Why are the folks always making a sacrofice out of lam in the old stories. What a mess.

Yours truly,
Chase
(age 10)

Dear God,

Do not worry about the starving peoples God. I will make sure the people in Ethiopa have plenty to eat and drink. I will save them my slami sandwiches from lunch and I will send it to them along with some vegtables. That will keep them from hunger for sure!

Love,
Therese
(age 9)

Dear God,

Let me in on something. Do you have a house keeper or do you clean up the world by yourself? There sure are a lots of crumbs around.

Andi
(age 11)

Dear God,

Please help my mom when she is cooking. Please watch over her. Last week she was making a pot roast and she almost cooked all of us. But she is a great mom and other kids should be so lucky, I think. I love her and I love you and my dad too.

Love,
Angie
(age 9)

Dear lord,

I pray to you every night. Right before I eat crackers and jelly and watch something stupid on tv.

Love to All,
Amelia
(age 7)

Dear God,

Chocolate is my favorite thing that you must have created. But I want to know which other things you magically made. What about chocolate chip cookies? Did you do that or did we come up with the idea on our own? It must have been a smart kid who thought that up. Its good for the milk business too, and it keeps Mrs. Fields working too.

Luv all the time,
Phillipa
(age 8)

Dear God,

I think it is amazin how many varities of food you have given us. Italian food is my personal choice for the best. I like all of them. Lasagne. Spagetti. Pasta. Ravioli. Chili. And Bagels. You make my stomach happy.

> Bye,
> Victor
> (age 11)

G, O, D,

I always spell your name in my alphabet soup.

> Violet
> (age 9)

Dear God,

Please come to our sedar meal at Passover. Each of us kids can invite a guest.

I think you will be okay but I will have to check with my parents.

> Talk with you,
> Jayne Z.
> (age 8)

Dear Jesus,

Did you turn to fishing since they have have less calories than meat?

> Lisa
> (age 11)

Dear God,

What did the people on Noah's Ark eat for food? Did they have to freeze everything?

Yours truly,
Anita
(age 9)

God,

Do you have feasts in heaven. We have feasts of St. Anthony and and St. Rosalie and others here.
Every person had a good time but the streets are a real mess the next day. Hope you are having fun too.

Love,
Sissela
(age 10)

Please send this strait to God,

I think you are great for all the wonderful things you provide. Toys, ganes, food. I try to not use them too much. Except for food. I have no control. I am fat. Sorry. I will try to do better.

Felicia
(age 9)

Dear god,

Lets have breakfast next Saturday. We can have orange juice naturally made by you and toast put in the toaster by me, Linda.

Linda,
(age 8)

To the God of the Jewish People,

Why do we get dry pancakes at Chanukah and the others get Christmas candy canes, chocolate and decent food? Did you want our stomachs to suffer of something?

> Yours truly,
> Dean
> (age 8)

Dear Father,

Please let us all have plente to eat. We want to thank you for all that dailee bread. And for being so kind and blessing the bread so it dont get mildew or moldee.

> Thanks,
> Geraldine
> (age 10)

Dear God,

I want to confess that I stole bubble gum from the 7 and 11 store last year. That was a long time ago but that was still bad. I want to tell you that I did not like the gum (it made me sick) and the baseball cards in it had no all stars. Mostly just guys from the Clevland Indians and the seattle team. So I was punished like I deserved.

> Please forgive me.
>
>
>
> (age 9)

Dear God,

I would like to share an ice cream with you some day. My favorite is pistashio. Yours must be heavenlie hash!

> Your friends,
> Glynnis
> (age 9)

For the Lord,

I pray to you just about every night around 9 O-clock. I also pray to you before every meal. I never even sneak a potato chip or a cookie first. This is no balonie either. Beleeve me.

> I have faith.
> Camille
> (age 10)

Dear God,

Could you change the laws and let kids drink wine for religious reasons. At least let the boys do it.

> Thanks
> Carl
> (age 11)

Dear God,

If the last supper was in the morning, would it be called the last breakfast?

I love Jesus very much and I wish that he did not have to suffer for our sins.

> Love,
> Kenneth
> (age 12)

Dear GOD,

When you decided to have Jesus say that the bread was his body that was a smart idea. But did you ever think of using cookies instead?

Sarah
(age 9)

Dear God,

If the Jews had micro waves when they left Egypt maybe the bread would of rose faster!

Sure thing,
Richard
(age 10)

Dear God,

You should visit us in Boston. We have seafood that is out of this world. You would like it since the fishes originally belonged to you.

Love,
Allan
(age 12)

Dear God, King of the Universe.

Lets eat stuff, drink a lot and be Mary. I know that is the way you want us to be. Like in the bible.

Best wishs,

Danny
(age 9)

Dear God,

I want to know what kind of cereal you eat in the morning. I eat frosted flakes and honey o cereals. I bet you must have bibleos. What is on the box? Proberly all the animals from the big ark.

Sherry
(age 7)

God,

I hate the taste of wine. Why didn't you have them drink fruit punch or papaya juice in Israel.

Love,
Michael
(age 11)

Dear God,

I am sorry. I like to do religious kind of things but fasting is where I draw the line. A man has to take a stand in life.

Neal W.
(age 10)

Dear God,

You are big and strong but you should not drink too much coffee or you will be up all year. I love a whole lot.

Love,
Andrea
(age 8)

For God,

In school we read about something called Manna or mannen or something like that. We read that the Bible characters really liked it a lot.

My question is did you put in any special ingrediants or artificial flavors. To make it taste better.

Or was it all natural?

Your friend and worshipper,
Anna
(age 10)

A message to God,

Please make sure all the starving folks in the world have
more. Give them lots of water and clothes too. And please
help me too.
       I am not always so great either. Sometimes I do not feel
good.

Thank you,
Keith
(age 8)

Dear God,

What day did you create food and clothing? I would like to
know what the first food was. I bet it was something you
could do quick like scrambled eggs.

Liz
(age 8)

Dear God,

Thanks for all the Christmas candy and cake. I did not get
sick this year.

Tim
(age 7)

8

Dear God,
Do You Have Freedom of
Speech in Heaven?

Dear God,

I am very full of thanks that you put me in the United States of America. Which is the land of the free and the home of the brave just like I bet you planned it. I am proud to be an American!

I bet if we lived in one of those curtain countrys we would have to pay taxes.

Made in the US,
Curtis
(age 11)

God—

Do you let the Devil (aileas Satan) go where he wants or do you keep tabs on him?

Cindy
(age 8)

Dear God,

You are a shepherd that I am not supposed to want. (I do not know what this means but we had a lesson about it last week).

Andy
(age 10)

Send to God,

I belief in you with out any douts at all. I like the way you are invisible so that we have to make up our own minds about you. Good idea.

                                              Love,
                                              Bo
                                              (age 10)

Dearest God,

I love you even when I have to say Hail Marys.

                                              Love,
                                              Ellen
                                              (age 6)

Dear God,

Do you let us decide things for ourselves or do just sit up there in the sky and dictate what you want.

                                              Either way,
                                              Your friend Carin
                                              (age 9)

Dear God.

Thank you for making sure that we have good laws to live by. That way we don't hurt each other.

                                              Dawn
                                              (age 10)

Dear God,

Why dont you let women do some of the same things men do
in the Bible?
    Except dieing as first born kids.

> How come.
> Gwen
> (age 8)

Dear God,

What do you do to relax? Can you take vacations in Florida?

> Bart
> (age 10)

Dear God,

I am glad that you let us choose what religions we are going
to be. One girl I know says she's in Christian Science. She
says her family does not care for doctors.
    I do not like them much either. I hate to go to them. And
dentists are even worst.
    Maybe I will find out more about her religion, if thats
okay with you.

> Your friend and letter writer,
> Jamie
> (age 10)

God,

Some people don't like to visit your house, but I do. Your house stands out. I like how you invite everybody but don't force anybody to come.

Love,
Allyson
(age 8)

Dear God,

I think it is great the way you are making Russia take it easy on the people and let them talk more. Now you should work on Africa and make them treat the peoples equal and the same down there in the south.

Jerome
(age 11)

To God,

Who does the world belong to? Do you have a contract in the sky that says you own it.

Louis, the Great
(age 10)

God,

Let us kids stay out after dark. (Or please make it dark much later)

Rich
(age 7)

Dear God,

Thanks for the air we breathe and the nice nature around like grass, which makes a nice decoration.

Charlie
(age 9)

Dear God,

Do you have freedom of speech in Heaven? Can people say anything they want about you.

Best wishes,
Tamara
(age 11)

Lord,

I'm glad that you have loosened up on going to church and that it is not demanded any more. Keep up the neat work.

Thanks,
Deana
(age 9)

Dear God,

Did you create baseball on the first six days or after on the day you rested. I hope you have time to catch a game once every now and then.

> Bob
> (age 9)

Dear god,

Do you have a queen? If not I think you should have a right to have one. You need a divine lady by your side.

> That's what I think,
> Jeff
> (age 10)

To the Lord the God,

In America we support freedom. That is why we support the Phillapines now. But I want to know if they are related to the Phillastines in the Bible. Are they?

> Stevie
> (age 9)

Dear God,

It must have been hard to watch what happened to Jesus. On the cross.

Did you have any second thoughts while it was going on. Could you have stopped it? Maybe you could have blown a big whissle or something.

> Bethany
> (age 11)

Dear God:

How do you select religions for people when they are born? Why did you make me a Catholic. Was it because I like Xmas and kids so much?

> Love,
> Marie
> (age 8)

God,

Who are you? How can we find you. You sure are difficult to pin down.

> Marti
> (age 10)

Dear God—

Can you show more control over kings and bishops and dictators. Some of them do not no what they are doing!

> Love,
> Sean
> (age 9)

DEAR MR. GOD,

No more plane crashes please. Let us fly to Hawaee and Porto Reco. . . . We are not ready to fly to heaven.

> Your friend & admirer,
> Kevin
> (age 8)

Dear God,

I want to know if you will let me make my own decissions for my self. Let's make a Deal.

I will sing in the choire at church and you let me go way away to Vermont next summer—with out my parents Joe and Cynthia Grich. Thank you. Let's shake on it.

OK?
Joseph Grich Jr.
(age 11)

Dear God,

You should exorcise your right for free speaking. You should have your own newspaper. That way you can talk to every person about what you are doing and about what they should do.

You can call it *God Today*.

GOOD LUCK.
ANGELA
(age 12)

God
Outside of Earth

Beam me up Scotty. I want to go home. I hope you saw Star Treks God. Can you make people disappear and reappear.

Mac,
(age 10)

Dear God,

Dont ever let the DEVIL out of jail! He's nothing but trouble.
I know first hand for a fact.

> Taylor
> (age 10)

God,

When you found Mary for the virgin birth and you decided
she would have Jesus in the manger, what I want to hear is
whether there were any other finalists?

> Hello God,
> Brittany
> (age 8)

Dear God.

Have you ever thought about giving human beings a choice
or two about when they rest in peace and die?
    You should. I would like to hang around till I am 237
years old. Then I would like to come and stay with you.

> See you then,
> Michael
> (age 9)

Dear God,

Do you travel much and write much or are you to tied up
with things like war, baby making, peace and confessions?
    Please write me when you can. I am busy with school but
I will read it.

> Ted
> (age 10)

Dear God,

Do you get free time to write letters to us humans? Just a short one would be great. I would want to no what average normal days are like for a god like you.

    Like how many bad guys do you round up and send downstairs.

Yours truly.
Peter
(age 9)

Dear GOD.

What happens if you a few bad things and say you are sorry, but are not sure if you really are?

    Does it matter if you are only 10?

Jan
(age 10)

God,

Who was that guy you put in the whale and then took out? Did he really agree to do that stunt?

Kaye
(age 9)

Dear God,

I do not know about other kids but I know I will love you and follow you and worship you and pray to you and respect you and think about you and bless you forever. And then some.

Kelly Anne
(age 8)

Dear God,

Do you have to be neutral about everything. Not play favorites. I understand if you do.
   If you don't, may be you could help the Red Sox. Look what happened to them in 86. Maybe you could make the wind stronger when they are hitting. That way they could hit lots of homers over the big green wall.

> A big fan of yours and
> the Red Sox,
> Kyle
> (age 9)

Dear God:

I just learned to use these two dots and the teacher said we are free to use them in our letters to you. So here they are.

> Love:
> Barry
> (age 10)

To God,

My dad told me it is okay to ask God for a favor. My dog Hulk died two months ago. Please take him into heaven and let him rome around. Without a leash. Don't worry. He won't run away. He is a good dog.

> Ellis
> (age 9)

Dear God,
You Must Have Been
Glad When You Finished
Coloring the Sky!

Dear GOD.

What is the best way to stay smiling? I want to know. If you tell me I promise not to be selfesh. I will share the news with every person on the earth.
    Even Gina, who is my older sister.

> Love,
> Roger P.
> (age 10)

God

Are there really angels? Do you have to be a girl? Can they really fly high?
    But can angels still do normal things like eat pasta and play soccor?

> You and the Pope are great,
> Georgio
> (age 9)

Dear God,

Wouldn't you be happier if every person could stop having angers and jealous ideas? That would make the world a better place.
    I sure hate hatred.

> Your buddy,
> Blaise
> (age 12)

Dear God,

It is summer but I wanted to say howdy. I am happy now
because I like to go to the beach and lay in the sun. I like to
swim and get a tan.

 You must be a great swimmer. I bet you can make all the
way around the Pacific Ocean and the Hudson River and the
East River. But you shouldn't try because you should not
swim in there. It is dirty.

Lorie
(age 10)

Letter to God,

How many Easter bunnies do you own? That must be fun
and you must make a lot of money at Easter.

Bye,
Hope
(age 7)

Dear God,

Christmas is the happiest day of the year. This is why I think
it must be. You have your front man, Santa Claus visit all of
us and making sure we are doing good. Then we get good
things even if we have been trouble makers all year.

See ya,
Robert
(age 8)

Dear Lord,

Thanks for the bike last Christmas Day. It has made me very happy except for May 13 at 4 o'clock when I rode into a big ditch that I did not see.

I am okay,
Spenser
(age 10)

Dear God,

I want to visit you in Paradise. Is there a big jet that goes there? Is it safe to travel? We just had a big crash around Detroit and I am afraid to fly. But I would be full of joy if I could see you.

See you soon,
Anita
(age 8)

Dear God,

I wish things were like they were many years ago. In the fun days. Those Romans knew how to live. The closest we come to that is football on Sundays.

Harry
(age 12)

God,

Was the sky difficult to color? Did you consider any thing else but blue? Maybe purple? Boy you must have been glad when you were finished coloring.

Barbara
(age 9)

Dear God,

My favorite sport is volley ball. I like it since you must hit it
to each other and that means you must get along with the
other players and you must have skill too. I think you should
create more sports like that so people will learn to get along
better.

The world would be more happy if all the adults and the
teenagers and the kids played volley ball. The grandmas and
grandpas can do something just like volley ball. Like play
Jim Rummy. That will make them feel good and will help
them be payshent with the others.

One girl's ideas,
Shannon
(age 9)

Dear God,

Do you like it best when you decide to have a new baby born
or when you save someone who is sick. Like they have cancer
or a cold. I would not like to have babies around so much.
They are yucky and cry a lot and have no hair. But it must
make you happy.

Jan
(age 7)

God of the Earth,

Hi. I want to say what a pretty world you made. The hills are
great and so are the ocean waters. I like to swim. You did a
good thing when you made beaches.

Luv,
Emily
(age 7)

GOD.

You could have all the posters in the world have your name
on them. Then you would not need to demand so much
worship since you would feel happy about your self.

Cory
(age 9)

Dear God,

Do you like Charlie Brown and snoopy? I do. They make me
feel like smiling. You should of put them in the Bible. They
Make good charackters!

I hope you do not mind this
    suggestion,
Erik
(age 8)

God,

It makes me feel glad so that you are watching us all the
time. That way we won't all go wild and crazy.

Your friend,
Pete
(age 9)

Dear God,

Is it better to get good grades in school or to be very nice to people. If you have to make a choice. Lets say maybe you are taking religion in Sunday school and the people you are talking about are ones you don't know. Atleast well. What is it better to do? What makes a person feel better?

Carl
(age 9)

To God,

What makes you tick, God? Since you created life you must have a good answer.

Sincerily,
Ernie, Grade 5
(age 11)

Dear Jesus,

Come on back. We really need you. And bring a sense of humor. You will need that!

Best wishes,
Cicely
(age 11)

Dear God,

Things are good in my family. It is two years since mom and dad were split. But I get along good with each now. I am sorry I was angry at them a long time ago. Please forgive me and thank you for pulling them apart and stopping their fighting. I hope we will still be a family you watch over.

With love,
Sari
(age 9)

Dear God.

God. Any time you are upset with all the war on earth and all the bad people just take a look at this. It will cheer you up.

Hi!
Marie
(age 11)

Dear God,

You must have been in a good mood when you made candy. I hope I never grow up. I love it. Only bad thing is that I have to take out the garbage or clean up in order to get allowence money for it.

Harold
(age 11)

To God!

What do you think about Whitney Huston? I figure she must be real pleased with her gold records and being admired by everyone.

Me. I would be satisfid with a chance to go to college when I grow up. That would make me pleased.

Please help, God
Kathy
(age 10)

Dear God,

I love most of all to visit parks and see the beautifil trees and
smell the pretty yellow flowers.
    You are definitly a super gardener.

                                                    Love,
                                                    Erica
                                                    (age 8)

Dear Father in Heaven.

Do you feed Santa Claus a huge meal on the night *before*
Christmas eve so that he will be extra jolly the next night?

                                                    Reed
                                                    (age 7)

Dear God,

I love it when you see to it that we come up with new
inventions. Our vcr is great. If they had that in Joshua's Day,
we could watch you make the sun stand still over and over
and over again.

                                                    Take it slow,
                                                    Scott G.
                                                    (age 11)

Dear God,

I hope to make it to your Kingdom and live it up.

                                                    Have a good day.
                                                    Linda
                                                    (age 11)

Dear GOD,

Christmas gives us good feelings and good times. Thanks. I am real pleased with the fine job you are doing.

Jackie
(age 7)

Dear God.

I feel that baptisms were the best idea so every one could be very religious and very happy. And they could be very clean too.

Love.
Sammy
(age 9)

Dear God.

The folk people in the Bible were always griping and complaning to you too much.
They should learn to smile more.

 Hank (Henry B.)
(Age 8)

Dear God,

I feel that people would feel good if they said more prayers and did not forget their prayers ever. I wish that older people and kids would prayer together more. That would make us feel like we are all part of the same generation. I feel that way since we are all children in your eyes.
Teach us to get our act together, God.

Love,
Virginia
(age 11)

Dear God,

If you gave the Jewish people their own land much sooner
they could have had more fun and they wouldn't have got
into so many troubles with the otherlands.

Steven C.
(age 8)

Dear god,

There should be a Christmas special about you.

Best wishes,
Joanne
(age 9)

God,

What is life for? I want to know what the purpose is.
    Let me know when you have a chance to figure out an
answer.

Sincerely,
Daniel
(age 11)

Dearest God,

What is your biggest wish? Mine is to have a thousand and
one dresses. Mostly red!

Joyce
(age 10)

Dear God,

I get happy when I touch people's noses and hug them. Your nose must be pretty big. Like a mountain.
Nobody better try to climb you in case you sneeze.

Jenna
(age 9)

Jesus,

you must have got a big smile on your face when you found out you was resurectered. I was glad when I heard about it too.

Luv,
Frank
(age 8)

Dear God,

Did you make clouds so you could tip toe down to earth?

Keep up the good work and
stay happy,
Jenny
(age 9)

Dear Jesus,

When you are with me I feel like everything is okay. Even great. Please watch over me. So everything can be great or even better.

Thank you.
Julia
(age 10)

Dear God,

I don't know where I would or could be without you and my
mother, Mrs. Carroll. My dad Mr. Carroll is okay too.

Steven K. Carroll
(age 9)

Dear God,

When a balloon goes high in the air does it get into heaven?
You must have a lot of nice ones up there with a lot of colors
on them.

Take it easy,
Patricia
(age 7)

10

Dear God,
How Big
Is Your Heart?

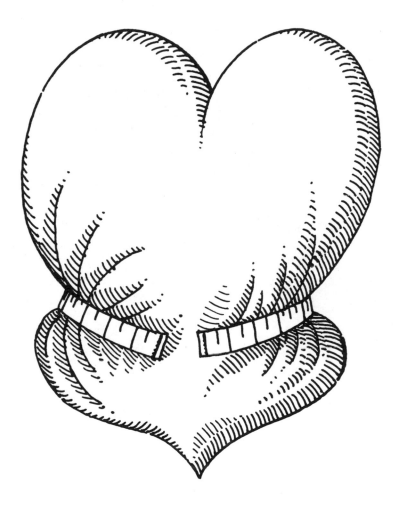

Dear God,

Who do you love the most? Jesus. Moses. Or Mary.
  I guess you may not want to say. But do not worry. I will
not tell them so that their feelings are not hurt.

Love,
Oliver
(age 8)

Dear god,

You are not a puzzle to me.

I got this from my mom,
Judy
(age 9)

A note for God,

WE ARE THE WORLD. We still love you even if it seems like
we don't.

Love,
Andrew
(age 8)

Dear God,

I am taugt to love my neighbors but some of the days I find
it hard. Please help me love old Mrs. Crayton even if she is a
crab.

Raymond
(age 10)

Dear God of War and Peace,

Why does the U.S. and the Soviet Unions not love each other
better?

Maybe you should make them love each other. You could
threatin them with hail storms and hurricanes and fire and
bugs.

That would convince them to love each other and reduce
nuclear weapons.

Martin
(age 11)

Dear God,

You should not be so high and mighty. You should be a
regular person and love us as equals. Not children or
servants. You should listen to me.

Andrea
(age 9)

Dear God, ♥

I love you all the time but I love you ten times as much at
XMAS!

Leigh
(age 6)

Dear GOD,

Do you have a crush on any female gods? Then you better watch your weight! Hah! Hah!

> Cool Pete
> (age 12)

Dear Sir,

I feel that it is great the way you pull the Jewish people out of trouble. Year in and year out.

You must love us and care about us a lot. Otherwise we would not be around any more.

> Thanks,
> Wendy
> (age 10)

Dear God,

Why do birds sing? My mom says it is cause they are falling in love. I think it is since you had them entertaining the other creatures on that Ark that Noah put together.

> Sincerely yours,
> Trevor
> (age 11)

God,

> You are neat.
> I wish I was.
> I am sloppy.
> But I love you.

> By,
> Allie
> (age 7)

Dearest God,

My folks tell me not to talk with strangers. But I will in your case because I like you so much. Bless you God.

Ryan
(age 9)

Dear Sweet God,

You are special.
I don't know another person or thing that could keep people going to church like you. I love you truly.

Louisa
(age 7)

Dear god

Happy Valatimes Day.

I would send you candy. I cannot. I do not have stamps.

Kendra
(age 6)

Dear God Man.

I feel you are an okay dude. U2 is a cool band. What kind of music do you like?
    I am into you even if you are far away.

Luv and rock and roll,
Bobby C.
(age 10)

Dear God,

Love was a very nice idea. Do you have any new ones? Keep trying.

> Taylor
> (age 11)

Dear God,

The Top Bible people you made was Moses, King Solomon and Romo and Juliet.

> That is my opinion,
> Jeri
> (age 10)

Letter to God,

What is the best way to love our brothers? Are 1st cousins also covered under this rule.

> Charlie
> (age 11)

Dear God,

I love you more than I can show from head to toe.
I am five inches more than four feet. Like I said I love you more than that.

> Your short friend,
> Jay
> (age unreported)

Hey God!

> Hello from a secret friend.
> Keep your chin up!
> Somebody down here loves you!

It's a secret,
(age 10)

Dear God,

Here's a true secret for only you and David Heller and the people who read his book.
PAM LOVES JIM. IT IS TRUE LOVE.
I am pam and Jim is my one and only lover. We are second graders. So don't make a big deal about it or we might get in trouble. Second graders are not supposed to love yet.
I am having a hard time keeping this in.

Luv,
Pam
(age 7)

Dear God,

Massachusets and Rode Island and New Hampshire and Maine all love you. So do the kids in Watertown. That is where I live.

With love from Watertown,
Harold
(age 9)

God,

When the Bible men fought hard, did you enjoy watching? I love wresling too. I especialy love a profesional wresler named Junkyard Dog. He is a big star.

> Demetrius
> (age 10)

Dear God,

Do the animals try to love each other the way we do? It must be pretty wild.

> T.R.
> (age 10)

Dear god,

Thank you for helping me when I was not picked to be class treasurer. I felt bad but you made me feel better. I love you a whole bunch for that.
    I feel fine now. I never liked money anyway.

> Thanks,
> Bobbi
> (age 11)

Dear God,

Teach us to love you better.
Maybe you could teach in the sixth grade or some other high level.

> Barrie
> (age 8)

Dear God,

I love you more than any body else that I do not know.

> Walt
> (age 10)

God,

Holy, holy, holy, holy—cow.
I beleive in you.

> Amen,
> Brian
> (age 11)

Dear God,

Love means never saying you are worried. You do not have to
worry when you believe in You, God.

> With loving kindness,
> Gloria
> (age 12)

Letter to God

Which of the beginning days was the one you created love
on? I think it was the first and my friend nicki thinks it was
the last. But could you rest and have love on the same day?!

> Love on all Days,
> Rachel
> (age 11)

Dear God,

You are kind and good. I am striving to be like you. I want to know if you have to love every person in order to be like you. That is hard for me.

Sincerely,
Catherine
(age 12)

To God. Where ever you are.

Come see me. I am sick with a thing called anemia. It means i get weak a lot. But I want to see you to make sure you love me as much as other kids.

Thank you sir,
Timothy, 7 Phillips Lane
(age 8)

God,

Love is all we need. (Along with bigger places to play).

Waylon
(age 8)

Dear Jesus,

I want to thank you for dying for our sins. I love you very much for that.
We sure do make a lot of sins here. Sorry. Maybe the next time that you visit we will be a little better.

Carol
With lots of love
and caring
(age 10)

Dear God,

How big is your heart?
Is it bigger than Europe or Canada?
Wow! You must be a real giant.

> Love,
> Barry
> (age 7)

Dear God,

We went to Niagara Falls this year. It is where my parents
went on their honeymoon. It is beautiful. Where do you go
for big trips like that?

> I try hard at praying &
> singing,
> James
> (age 9)

To God,

What is your favorite romantic movie? I used to like Return
of the Jedi but now I like a love story called *Who is that girl*.

> Benita
> (age 10)

God,

Love is a 2 way Street.
Its your turn, God! Help!
I just want to know you are there.

> Tiffany
> (age 10)

Dear Jesus,

Ever since I was five I have been a big fan of yours. Now that I am 3 years older and I have all these years under my belt, you can count on me for bigger things.

Love,
R.C.
(age 8)

Dear God,

Do you love sports the way I do. I think you must. Thats why you created baseball diamons and football fields. And you also made the balls to go with it.

Love all the time
Carlton
(age 9)

Dear God,
You Should Have a Big
Microphone and Loud
Speakers So We Can
Hear You Better!

Dear God,

I was just thinking. What do you make of this Glassnose thing? I don't understand this Russian stuff.

Andrew
(age 11)

Dear God,

I always tell the truth when I can. If it is going to hurt some ones feelings, is it best to tell the truth all the time?

I dont mean a big lie or anything,
Sherry
(age 9)

Dear God,

Do you root for Noter Dame since they are a religion school. I like colleges very much. My teams are Michigan (cause I live there) and Miami (cause I like there uniforms). I think maybe they play Noter Dame. But they are not in the same leage. They're stadiums do not have churches right on top of them.

Your friend,
Christopher
(age 10)

Dear god—

I have no false ones before you.
I swear it.

> With total belief.
> Everett
> (age 10)

Dear god,

People (mostly dumb kids in my homeroom) say I have a
funny nose. Do you think I do?

> Thank you,
> Ted
> (age 8)

Dear god;

Help us choose the right president.
Help America be strong.
Help us make peace with russia.
Help us win the Olympics.
Help us not to depend on money so much.

> Sincerely,
> Gerald
> (age 12)

Dear God,

Do you have any say about who gets elected here. Please
make sure some of the states go to the democrats. They have
not done too well in a long time.

> Best wishes to you,
> Gayle
> (age 11)

God,

You are the God for all the persons of the world. I know it for
a fact. When we went to Europe and France all the people
worshipped you.
　　I just thought you might like to hear about it.

　　　　　　　　　　　　　　　　　　　　Nancy
　　　　　　　　　　　　　　　　　　　　(age 8)

Dear God,

I know that you are easy to talk to since I talk to you every
night when I pray. I just want you to know that I think about
you during the day too.

　　　　　　　　　　　　　　　Take care and do your great
　　　　　　　　　　　　　　　work,
　　　　　　　　　　　　　　　Eli
　　　　　　　　　　　　　　　(age 11)

God/Jesus.

I have a box where I keep all my valuabled things and stuff.
I want to let you know that I have my cross there.
　　You did not die for nothing.

　　　　　　　　　　　　　　　　　　　　Joe
　　　　　　　　　　　　　　　　　　　　(age 10)

My God,

You are good and kind. Every man should give you what you
deserve. A WHOLE LOT OF FAITH.

　　　　　　　　　　　　　　　　　　　　Love,
　　　　　　　　　　　　　　　　　　　　R.D.
　　　　　　　　　　　　　　　　　　　　(age 9)

Dear God,

I like to go on vacations. It is great. I can stay up late.
    Did the Bible peoples take to the deserts and the oceans
too. They should have. They could have more relaxing and
have fewer wars that way.

                                                    Sharon
                                                    (Age 8)

God,

Thank you for the wind which
helps me to fly my kite.

                                                    Love,
                                                    Marie S.
                                                    (age 9)

Dear God,

My best movie is Gone In The Winds.
Did you ever get to see it?
Do you ever see our pictures?
Most have too much war and sex.
But not Gone In The Winds.

                                                    Tracy
                                                    (age 9)

Dear god.

Please help me to be on time more of the time. Last week I was even late to basketball practice. I could get benched for that.

> Thank you,
> Jim
> (age 11)

Dear God,

Say hello to Jesus for me. I try hard to listen to your ideas and choose the ones that are best for me.

> with much love,
> Melissa
> (age 9)

Dear, Hashem (God),

My wish is for Israel not to have any more troubles with its neihbors.
Neihbors should keep off each others propertys. Maybe they should put up a fence. Thats what the people down the block did when their neibors dog kept going on the lawn.

> I care about this,
> Beth
> (age 10)

Dear GOD,

You should have a big religious holiday in August. It is very hot and dull here then.

> Art
> (age 9)

Dear Holy God,

How did you come up with the idea of marriage. I believe in
the sanction of marriage. Do not get me wrong. I am
Catholic. But did you ever think about having more than two
live together.
    I guess not. I would not be a marriage then.

> Bye bye.
> Carol
> (age 12)

Dear God,

I am angry with you, God. We have to move all the time. My
father gets transferred all the time. I have to leave my
friends and get real sad. I want to believe more in you but
how can I when you make us move all the time.

> Elizabeth
> (age 11)

Dear god,

I do not know how to swim. Could you help me learn? That
way you wouldn't have to part the water every time I go in.

> Please,
> Jamie
> (age 7)

To god,

I pray to you before every swim meet. I like to win. So does my friend Julie. She prays too. But I always beat her. Does that mean you like me best or you don't care about swimming?
    Maybe she should win at least 1 or 2 times.

Love.
Missy
(age 11)

God,

I like science. I specialy like to study fossels, and rocks and mountains. Someday I would like to climb Mount Sinai with you!

Very truly & Love,
Nate
(age 10)

Dear God,

You made great fruits and vegtables!
We eat them all the time.
I really like carrot cake best.

Thank you.
Cody
(age 8)

Mister GOD,

Why don't you buy a big microphone and loud speakers so
that we can hear you better down here?

> Think about it, please. We really
> need some changes.
> Alexander S.
> (age 10)

Dear God,

What did you think about that movie about Jesus called
Temtations.
    I thought it stunk even tho I didnt see it.

> Jason
> (age 9)

God,

Why did you make the moon? Did it catch you off guard
when we made it up there?

> Love,
> Todd
> (age 10)

Dear God,

I know that you are made of all kinds of people. When I
suggested this in religious school my teacher told me I was
wrong. You should be more careful about who you hire to
teach your stuff.

> Yours truly yours,
> Marci
> (age 11)

Dear God,

I think of you when I ride the train. Which is also called a railroad. Because it takes me to far away places. I think you live in a far away place called heaven.

I do not know if the train could ever find a way to go there.

Elaine
(age 8)

Dear God,

I have many favorites. You are my best religious person. My favorite guy in music is eltons jon. My baseball favorite is named Mookie. So you are part of a good company.

Love,
Delia
(age 7)

Dear Wonderful Lord,

What do you think of brand names on clothes and dresses. I think they are so stupid.

That's all for now,
Tina
(age 10)

DEAR GOD,

Tell the truth. Did you really preform all those miracles yourself?

Love & Kisses,
Ellie
(age 9)

Hi God!

I think you should think as much about giving as a person thinks about taking things. That is why I am putting YOU on my christmas shopping list.

Angela
(age 11)

To God,

Thanks for helping me out of that jam in social studies. My grades will get better now. You are a true life saver.

Cris
(age 10)

dear god,

Whats happening up there where you push all the buttons?

See ya,
Terrence
(age 10)

Dear Friend,

I know you care about me God. That makes me feel good even if I don't feel so good about my self.

Love always,
Amanda
(age 8)

Dear God,

How do you find a mom and dad for each kid? Do you match them up by their religions, what colors they are or by cities?
Or maybe something else very different. Maybe you just use a big lottary.
I must have won kind of but my friend Billy did not do so good. Please help him.

Love,
PAUL
(age 9)

Dear Lady God,

I love you. And I want to thank you making the color pink. Pink is a beautiful creation.
I think in heaven you must have made lots pink. Pink cushons, pink houses, even pink clouds.
I just hope that the boys dont feel too out of place. That would be too bad.

I love you lots.
Liz Marie
(age 7)

Dear God and Your disipels,

Please forgive me for not being a better listener at church. But it is hard to learn about you all at once.

Hello.
Carmen
(age 10)

Dear god,

Good morning Heaven! How are you today? I am fine. The
sun is shining and people are doing fun things.
     Very good!

Love,
Molly
(age 6)

Dear sweet god,

You are where I want to be after I am gone. But for now I like
it here.

Love,
Candace
(age 9)

Dear God,

Lets keep in touch.

Love,
Gregory
(age 12)